ALFRED HOLLINS

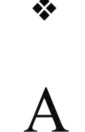

A
TRUMPET
MINUET

FOR ORGAN

To my friend John K. Young.

A TRUMPET MINUET

Solo (Top Manual) Orch. Trumpet coupled
to Swell with no stops drawn.
Accompaniment on Great in proportion.

Alfred Hollins

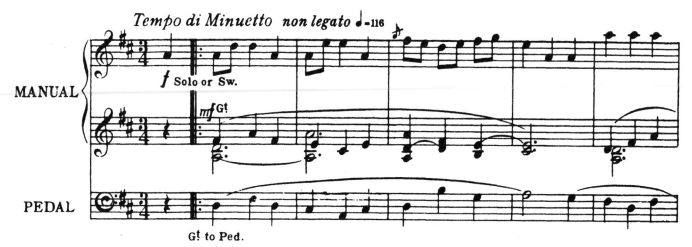

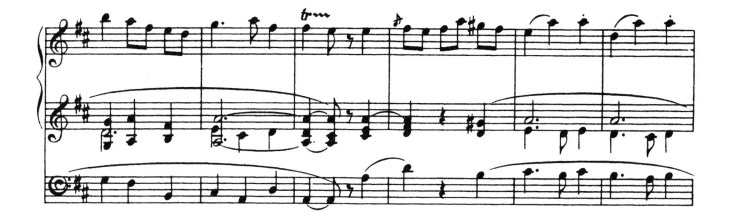

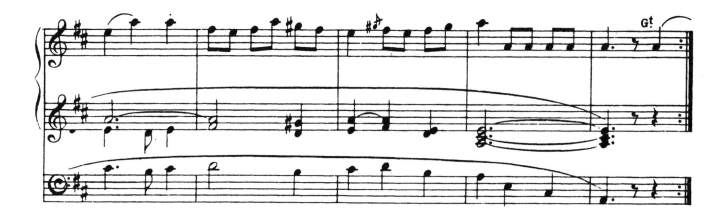

15535

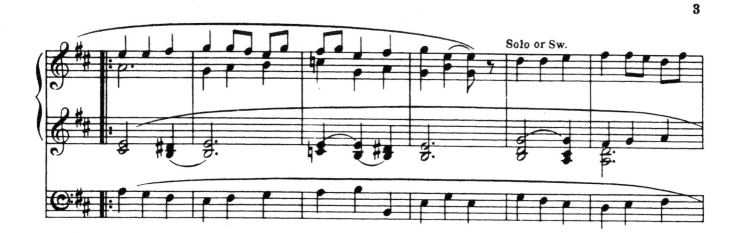

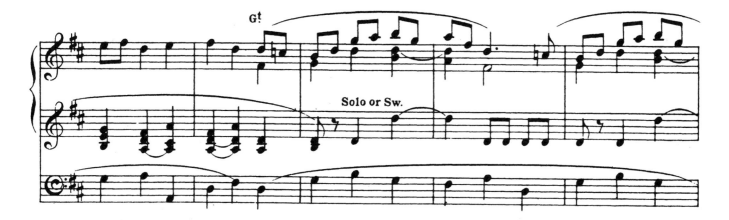

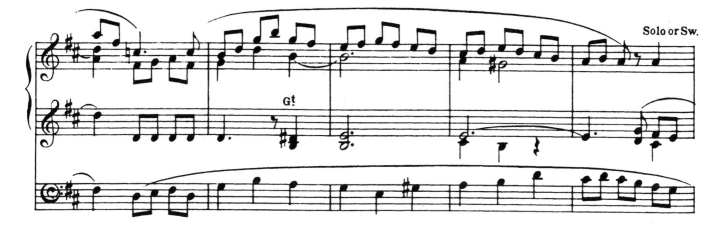

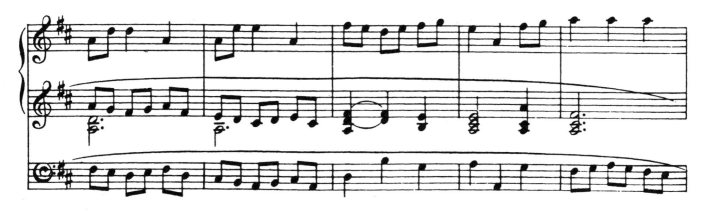

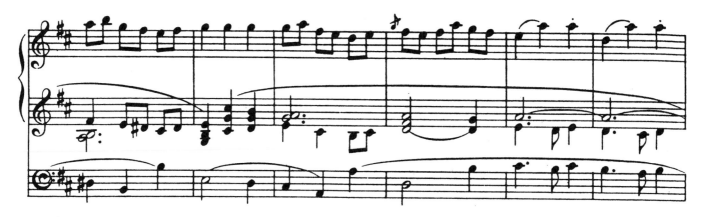

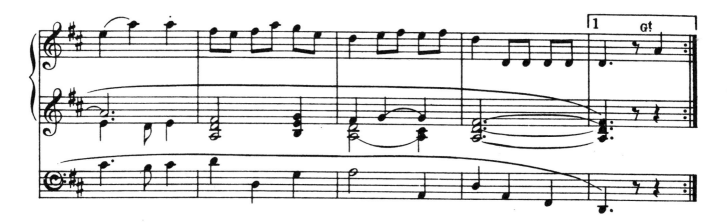

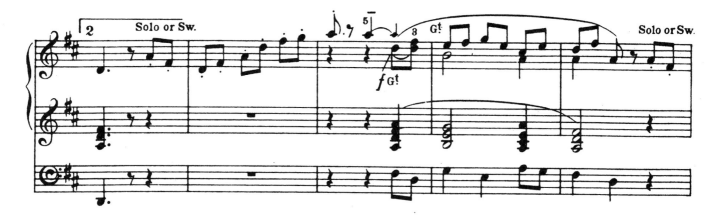

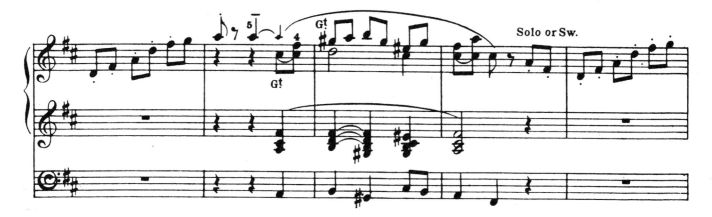

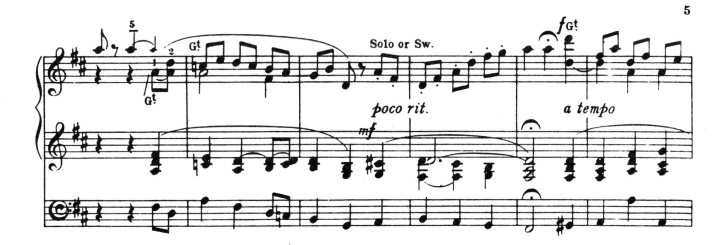

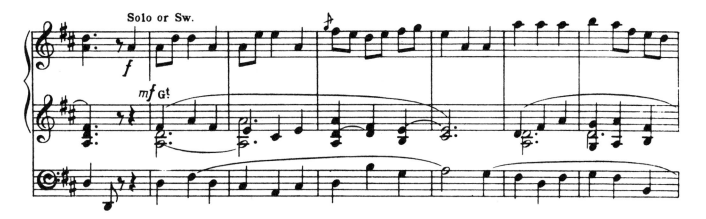

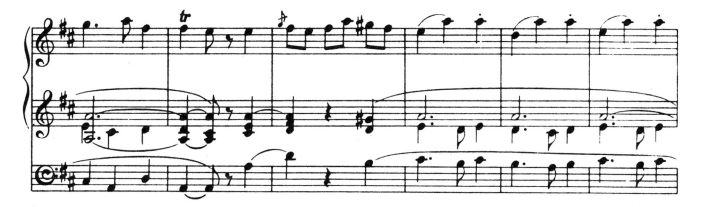

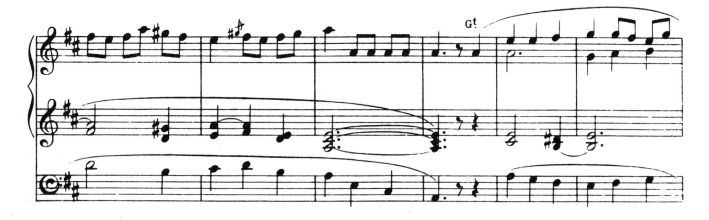

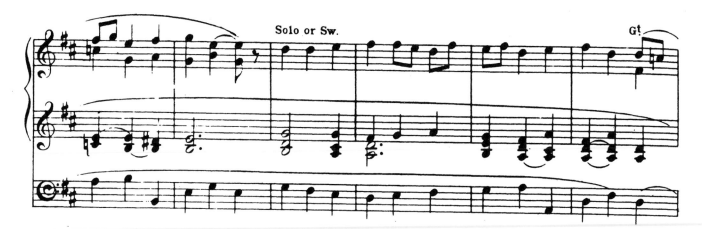

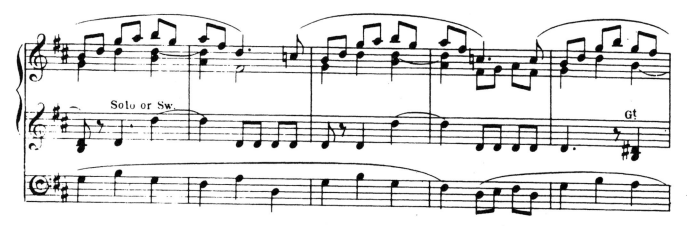

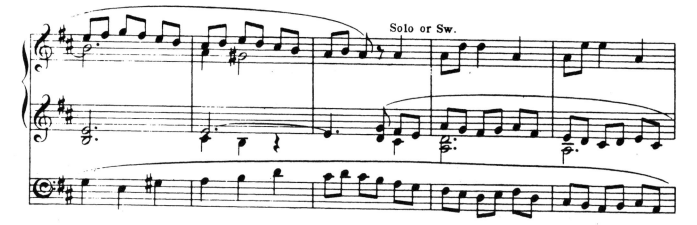

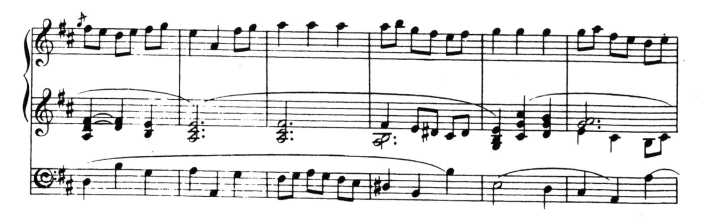

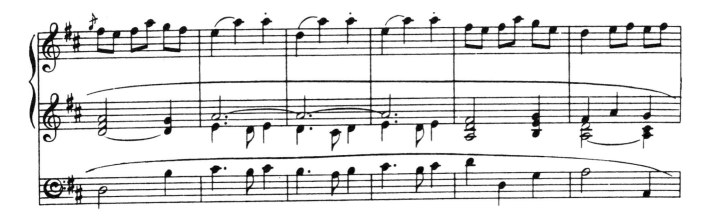

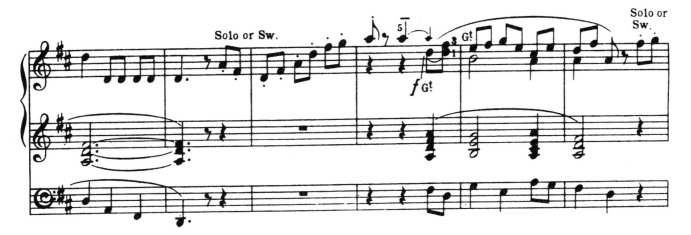

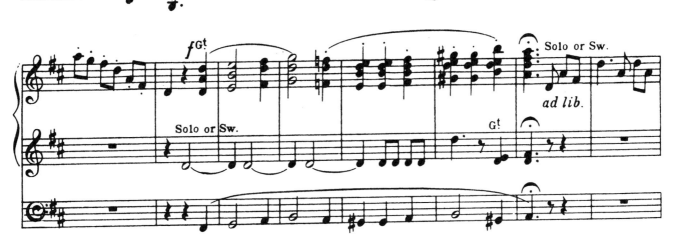

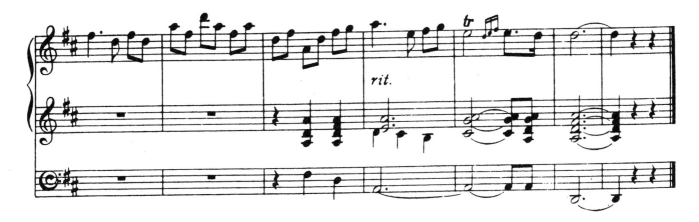